From Beauty School to Boss

Tracey A. Hardaway

Copyright © 2020 Tracey A. Hardaway

All rights reserved.

ISBN:

Dedication

I'm too old. I will be behind in the class. I will be the oldest person in class. I won't be able to keep up with the young folks. It will take too long to graduate. I don't have enough time to do this after working all day. We don't have enough money for this. Who will take care of the kids? Where am I going to work after I graduate? I don't have the energy. What will "they" think about me?

This list of excuses is just a sample of what I said to my husband Terrance when I was deciding to make a step toward my purpose. I said these things to him when I was considering enrolling in cosmetology school and later when deciding to open my own salon. I have a few of these excuses going through my head now – as I am writing this book. I dedicate this book to him because with every excuse I gave, his response was always the same - - YOU CAN DO IT. Not only did he love me, encourage me, and give me confidence when I had none, he also stepped up and took care of whatever needed to be done for me, our children, and the business, regardless of his health. As a working mother, I would sometimes feel sad and guilty for missing some of my kids' activities, and he would always remind me that our children have two parents and that he was not only willing but was able to take care of them when I was not there. And in some ways, he was even better at it than me. For that, I am truly grateful and blessed. I love you for loving me.

Contents

Acknowledgments 1

Preface 2

1 Set the Tone 6

2 Your Website 12

3 Community 16

4 Communication 17

5 Training 19

6 Collaboration 22

7 Location 24

8 Encouragement 29

About the Author 35

Acknowledgments

I want to thank all of my clients for trusting me with their hair. Some of you have been with me for many years. I hope that I met and exceeded your expectations. We have laughed, cried, disagreed, debated, and watched our children grow. Your time with me is priceless. To my children Taylor and Tristan. You have been the energy I needed at the end of a long day; the confidence I needed to pursue my dreams; and the motivation I needed to continue when I wanted to quit. I love you beyond time.

Preface

This book is being written while we, as a nation and especially as beauty professionals, have been significantly impacted by the COVID-19 pandemic. I, like you, had to adhere to the safer-at-home quarantine that required me to temporarily close my salon. Many beauty professionals were unexpectedly left without any income to sustain their businesses or to provide for their families. Fortunately, I built my businesses on the principles I teach in this book. Having these processes in place prepared me to immediately reopen my business without making any drastic changes in business or to my customers' experience. I hope that each of you have been able to grow during this uncertain time and that what I am sharing with you in this book will help you better position yourself for the next "unexpected" change.

> WHAT IS A BOSS? Definition:
>
> A person who knows what he or she wants, knows how to get what he wants, and gets it when he wants. He or she lives by his or her own code and does not care about what others think. A boss has his or her own personality, and does not follow the norm, just because it is the norm. A boss does not settle for less than what he or she is worthy of.
>
> -Urban Dictionary

My Story

Getting my cosmetology license was one of the best decisions I've ever made. If someone had said to me back then that one day I would take all of my lessons learned, research, successes, and failures and become a coach for independent beauty professionals, I would have laughed and called them crazy. Thirteen years later, here I am helping others--like you--pursue a bigger dream. I now teach beauty professionals not only how to own a salon but also how to take their unique skills and services to create revenue streams that extend beyond the salon.

I know what you're thinking... "Tracey, I don't have enough time in my day to do what I already need to do, let alone do even more!" I understand what you're saying. I used to say that too.

Does this sound familiar?

I don't have enough time to...

1. Take care of my family (a husband and 2 young children):
2. Work a full-time job;
3. Develop my skills to become a certified non-surgical hair replacement specialist; and
4. Run a service-based business at the same time.

But you know what? What I said could not happen is exactly what I made happen.

You see, while I was living what looked like the American dream with a great family, good paying job, nice home, etc.; I was not fulfilled. I knew God had something else for me to do. That something was always there, but I would push it aside and make excuses for not going for it. All of that changed when I asked my supervisor for a raise after working 15 years on the job.

Now, in case you can't tell, I am a hard worker and a go-getter-always have been, always will be. As the daughter of two poor, hard-working parents and the youngest of five siblings, how could I not be? When I walked into my boss' office and asked for a raise, I did not go empty handed. I presented him with a list of all of the tasks I had completed in my position as a government administrator and everything I was willing to do for advancement, so I just knew his response was going to be, "How much do you want?" I was wrong. His response, instead, was, "Tracey, this job pays what it pays, and there is no room for promotion. If you don't like it, you can go back to your old job."

Needless to say, this was like getting a punch to the gut. I felt as if everything I had worked for meant nothing. That was the catalyst for months of depression. When I finally regained my footing--after putting my family through undeserved stress--my husband encouraged me to do what I had talked about doing for years--become a cosmetologist. I took his advice, and I enrolled in cosmetology school, took classes at night, and within two years of working during the day and attending classes at night, I graduated and got my cosmetology license.

I know this sounds funny and maybe even strange, but my spirit leaped when I did my first roller set. It really did! I knew I had found my purpose. Once you've found your purpose, you'll understand. You'll just know when you've taken that first step in the right direction. In fact, I didn't just walk in the right direction…. I ran.

While I was in cosmetology school, I felt as if I couldn't absorb the information fast enough. I was the first one to raise my hand in class and to volunteer to try new techniques. I even purchased books and videos to study and practice at home. I was "all in." However, this newfound purpose also created a newfound problem. How was I going to walk "in purpose" and continue to provide for my family?

The obvious answer was to "step out on faith" and quit my job to do hair, right? Wrong. This may have been the obvious answer; but it was not the best answer for my family. You see, while I was going through my professional struggles, my husband was going through a serious health struggle and he had to liquidate his business. Consequently, we needed my steady income and benefits. I knew if I were going to pursue my dream in the real world, I had to get creative.

I was motivated by one goal--to create a business model that would simultaneously work for me and my family and meet a need in the hair industry. I gravitated toward something I know - hair loss. You see, I have trichotillomania, so I understand hair loss and the embarrassment women feel when getting their hair done in open-concept salons. Understanding my customer allowed me to meet this need by offering privacy and one-on-one services.

Hair Candy Salon, Your Extension Suite

The solution? Hair Candy Salon, Your Extension Suite. I help women who are dealing with various types and degrees of hair loss get their salon needs met in a professional and private environment.

After over 13 years of helping many amazing women from all backgrounds, races, ages, and cultures, my purpose has evolved to meet an additional need in the industry. I now provide help for beauty professionals who want to take the next step in their careers-- the same type of help I wish I had received when I started. Don't get me wrong. I still love doing hair, but I also love being able to give back to a profession that has allowed me to grow spiritually, personally, professionally, and financially.

Listen, this journey has not been easy, but it certainly has been worth it. There is no straight line to success but once you get there, it's an indescribable feeling. In fact, I remember the moment I got my own salon like it was yesterday. I was scared. I was excited. I knew the possibilities for growth were endless. If you're reading this book, perhaps you have unmet goals. It only takes one step in the right direction to get closer to your dream. I want to be the example that helps you take that first step. If you're ready to get started, read on. I am going to share 7 actions that will help transform your dreams into reality.

1 SET THE TONE

Action 1 - In business and, even in life, you must set the tone...

I was blessed to have an amazing cosmetology instructor. At times she was not nice, but she knew her stuff and I respected that. One lesson she taught stuck with me, and I live by it today. It is so important that I want you to adopt the same philosophy.

You may have heard the phrase, "set the tone". In business, it simply means the quality, feeling, or attitude you convey when speaking or writing. The good news is that this is something entirely in your control. My cosmetology instructor taught our class that our clients are often a reflection of ourselves. In my years in business and as a wife, mother and employee, I find this to be true in many ways. The bible puts it another way in Proverbs 18:24. It says, **"A man who has friends must himself be friendly."**

As you are preparing to start your beauty career or transition to open your own business, I encourage you to take a moment to evaluate yourself by answering the following questions:

What do you watch on TV?

Why do you do what you do?

What do you say about yourself?

How are you living?

What do the people closest to you say about you?

Where do you see yourself 5, 10, 15, or 20 years from now?

When I am consulting with new professionals, the main thing they struggle with is setting their prices. They have been taught that - since they are just starting out, they should price their services low and raise them as they gain more experience. I totally disagree with this practice because - as creatives, time does not equal quality of work. This is why setting the tone is so important. New beauty professionals often know in their gut that they should charge more. However, they are often afraid to ask for more money because they believe what they were told by someone who was told that same thing when they started their careers. John Hope Bryant, the author of one of my favorite books "Up from Nothing", mentions that as entrepreneurs and creators, WE are our most valuable product and we are worth our price.

You must set the tone at the start of your career by pricing your goods and services based on what you know they AND you are worth. This can only be determined by YOU. Of course, you must research the market in your area and go from there.

If you are the best - Say So

As you research, don't make the mistake of comparing yourself to others. You are your own competition. Strive to be the best in what you do and if you are the best, say so - you will be paid accordingly.

Here are some examples:

- Do you offer special techniques?
- Is this service limited in your area?
- Do you have extra/advanced certifications?
- Do you have testimonials of high-profile or highly-exposed people that use your services?
- Do you have proof of concept (e.g. show hair growth by using your products and techniques) and can show this proof to potential customers?
- Are you meeting a specific need you can clearly communicate to your customers?
- Do you teach what you know to others by conducting workshops or online tutorials?

How you answer these questions will help you not only decide your price structure, but it will also give you the confidence to ask for it without fear or hesitation. Communicating your worth is part of setting the tone of your business.

> The primary reason some beauty professionals struggle with pricing their services is because they have not clearly defined why they do what they do and who they do it for.

When I ask beauty professionals this question, the answer is most often to provide for their families. If this is truly the reason, then I ask them why they think their time away from their family, providing a service is not worth 10 or 20 more dollars. This is often an eye-opening frame of reference that puts a different perspective on why they do what they do. It also breaks down any barriers or fears of charging what they know they truly deserve.

Of course, we beauty professionals love the beauty industry and all that comes with it, but ultimately - we all want to be compensated for our time and expertise. I don't know about you, but when I am done working at the salon for the day, I am completely exhausted because I have poured all of myself into my creation and into making sure I have over delivered for my customer. That feeling is priceless.

> However, to attract customers that want what you create, you must first know—without a doubt—that you deserve to be compensated for it.

In essence, you must set the tone.

Everything I have written about in this book starts with setting the tone and sharing who you are and what you offer through your website, how you engage with your community, how you communicate verbally and non-verbally, your expertise and continued education, your collaboration (partnerships), and even your location. All of these factors allow you to set the tone for your business and go from beauty school to boss.

2 YOUR WEBSITE

Action 2 - You are the Product...

The first step to getting people into your chair or business is to let them know that you exist. Your customers need to know who you are and why they need you. The best way to do this is with your website. Most beauty professionals rely on others to create a website for them - which is totally fine. This is better than not having a website at all. Whether you plan to hire someone or do it yourself, you need to make sure that your website clearly defines who you are and how you can help meet your customer's needs. It should include:

- Home Page
- Services Page
- Purpose
- About
- Helpful Tips and Tools
- Social Links
- Contact

Your website may be your initial introduction to your customers, so make it look as great as possible.

Home Page - The Home Page is the most important page on your website. It is your initial introduction to your customers, so make it look as great as possible and provide the following:

- Tell them exactly what you do and why they should book with you.
- Tell them how you will solve their problem.
- Tell them what they need to do next.

Services Page - Here is where you will list all of your services, but go a step further and describe how the clients will benefit from your services. Here is an example of a great description:

> I give you a precision cut so that you save time getting dressed for work.

Purpose - I cannot say enough about the purpose page because here is where you tell your customers why you do what you do. Don't rush through this one. You are not selling to everyone. Remember, you want to attract your ideal customer. More than likely, this will be someone who has similar tastes and values as you.

About - This page is almost as important as your purpose page. This is where you will talk about yourself. There is no need to give your life story; just make sure it is relatable to your ideal customer.

Helpful Tips and Tools - Attracting your ideal customers means you are going to have to give some things away. This is called "added value." Provide a list of how to's, product referrals, videos, etc. This not only helps your customers, but it also shows that you are an expert in what you do.

Social Links - Add all of your links to your site and make sure that they automatically update as you post them through your phone or other devices.

Contact - Make it easy for them to find you by embedding Google Maps, text, email, online schedulers, etc.

Now that I have told you what should be on your website, here is a list of easy DIY Web hosting services that make it easy for you to get your website up and running and looking beautiful:

Wix.com

Godaddy.com

Squarespace.com

If you decide to hire someone to create/design your website, I recommend you draw out exactly what you want it to include. Remember, they work for you so don't settle for less than you want. You are the creative professional, and this site may be the first impression your potential customer will receive of you. And it will have your name on it. Here is a list of sites that I personally use to make my websites pop:

Canva

Pixistock

Pixaby

Smart Mockup

Creative Market

Namecheap

3 COMMUNITY

Action 3 - Tell people you know and don't know what you do...

In order to attract your ideal customer and grow your business, you must put yourself out there. A great way to do this is through community engagement events. Research your local area for community events that your ideal customers frequent. Don't just show up, engage, volunteer, participate. Be observant, take notes, and notice how you may be able to help potential clients with your offerings. If you cannot find the right event, host an event yourself for the benefit of your community.

Here are a few types of community engagements to consider:

Charity Marathons

Sororities and Fraternities

Community Building Projects

Job Fairs

Local Business Centers

Area Chamber of Commerce

School Career Days

4 COMMUNICATION

Action 4 – Always be selling...

There are four forms of communication: verbal, non-verbal, written, and visual. You must learn to use all of these forms of communication to attract your ideal customer and to sustain and grow your business. If you want to be successful - keep these 3 words in mind:

Always Be Selling

This cannot be truer for beauty professionals. Every time you leave home, you must be selling your product. Remember, the product is YOU. Here are 2 examples of what I mean.

> **Example 1:**
>
> You are in line at Chick-fil-A, and you see someone who fits the profile of your ideal customer. Traditionally, you would walk up to this person, hand him or her a business card, and ask to give you a call if they need **XYZ**.

In this example, there is a 50/50 chance that they will call… if you're lucky.

But, if you are aware of the four forms of communication the best one for beauty professionals is visual. If done correctly, visual communication is neither annoying nor intrusive. If you beautifully represent what you are selling AT ALL TIMES your customers will be attracted to you. See Example 2.

> **Example 2:**
> You are in line in Chick-fil-A, and you see someone who fits the profile of your ideal customer. You stand in line as close to them as possible, and start a conversation about the menu or the weather - - not about what you're selling. This breaks down their barriers and gives them the opportunity to see you (visual and non-verbal communication) and your hair, make-up, braids, nails, skin, etc. This will open the door for the other two forms of communication, which will allow you to tell (verbal) what you do and provide (written) your contact information without you selling them.

They are sold by how you
represent you and your brand.

5 TRAINING

Action 5 – Each one, teach one...

The saying, "Each one, Teach one" is a proverb that originated in America during slavery times. Slaves were denied an education so when one slave learned to read or write, it became his duty to teach someone else. Frank Laubach, a Christian missionary, went on to use the phrase to address poverty and illiteracy in the Philippines. I believe in this principle as well.

It is our duty to educate others for the good of the industry.

Simply put, as we learn concepts, strategies, techniques, etc., I believe it is our duty to educate others for the good of the industry.

Get as much training as you can. Learn as much as you can. Computers and cell phones - coupled with the internet, have made learning extremely accessible and easy. Many successful entrepreneurs and influencers are self-taught. The fact that you have purchased this book tells me that you already know the value of education and the importance of training.

If you've graduated from cosmetology school, the real education and training begins after you've earned your license. If you have opened a business, the real education and training begins when you open your doors and sometimes, when you close them as well.

After graduating beauty school and opening my salon, I used the internet to find all of the training I could afford. In 2006, YouTube was not as popular for instruction, so I purchased magazines, videos and books. And I practiced, practiced, practiced to perfection. I am still learning in every way possible.

Do not let a lack of licenses, certifications, and/or training stop you from learning and teaching what you have learned to others. The beauty industry is built on creativity. You don't need a license, degree, or certification to create and teach.

Research popular magazines such as Glamour, Vogue, Essence, Shape, Cosmopolitan, etc., and read the editorial pages (found in the back) to see who styled the models. Research each stylist and find out where they are located or if they offer training. Be bold and send them a direct message on their platforms. Also, if you attend trade conferences, research attending platform artists and follow their social platforms for training opportunities. Make the necessary investments that will advance your skills.

+Get and give as much training as you can. While YouTube is great for learning, it is also one of the best ways to grow your skills and customer base by teaching. Create a channel to draw attention to your talents and your business. You never know what celebrity, producer, director, etc., may be watching. This will help you to establish yourself as an expert in your field.

When you teach you learn as well, and you become more knowledgeable of your subject. When you learn a new technique, process, or even try products - - teach it to someone else. This process will help make you better and help someone else as well.

6 COLLABORATION

Action 6 – Connect to something bigger than yourself...

When you are starting out and trying to grow your business, it is important to connect to something bigger than yourself. By "bigger" I mean, non-profit organizations and/or corporations. It is great to have a million followers on social media, but growing a business takes more than followers; it takes buyers. People are looking for a particular service that will solve their problem and/or meet a need. One way to meet a need or solve a problem is through collaboration.

> *Everyone gets the same 24-hour day.*
> *You just might be the help someone needs.*

In order to be found on search engines, it helps if you are affiliated with well-known organizations. For example, I told you that I started my salon with zero money and clientele. One of the primary ways I was able to be found and ranked high with search engines like Google was by joining organizations that catered to a niche market. Some of them were free to join while others required an annual membership fee. I was able to join large organizations as a service provider in my area. This collaboration/affiliation pushed me up in Google searches and affiliated me with organizations that people already know, like and trust. Examples of these are:

American Hair Loss Council
American Cancer Society
Children with Hair Loss
The TLC Foundation
(Trichotillomania - Hair Pulling Disorder) Hair Visions International

Contact that artist you have been stalking on social media and ask to partner with some of their projects or offer to help them in meeting some of their customer demands. Remember, everyone gets the same 24-hour day. You just might be the help someone needs.

7 LOCATION

Action 7 - Where there is a will, there is a way...

I saved location for last because where you choose to start your career or open your business is crucial. Your location is the foundation upon which your business will stand and grow.

I mentioned (in my story) that I opened my salon immediately after getting my cosmetology license in 2006 before the salon suite chains like Sola Salons and Phenix salon suites became popular. I had no clientele, no experience, and very little money.

The truth is, I actually started looking for my own salon location before graduating cosmetology school and getting my license. And so should you.

> *Your location is the foundation upon which your business will stand and grow.*

The decision to start my career this way did not come easily. Like you, I attended the job fairs, took the tours, did the shadowing, etc.

None of these options worked for me because I could not quit my steady job (with benefits) to work as an assistant stylist and work my way up. Remember - - I did not have clientele, so renting a booth/chair part-time did not make sense - - nor could I afford it. I had to create a location that worked for me. This is what you may have to do in order to build your business on a solid foundation. Finding a location is easier than you think if you are willing to think outside of the box - or in this case - the traditional salon environment.

This is what I mean: Brick-and-mortar spaces are becoming more and more available with the creation of online retailing. Using the principles taught here, you now know…

- Who you are;
- What you offer;
- You are always selling by consistently presenting yourself as a business owner;
- You are an educator and, therefore, an expert in your craft; and
- You are connected to a community where you not only receive but you also give.

Now look for spaces, salons, suites, etc., that will let you showcase YOU. If you cannot find one already created, you have what it takes to create it for yourself, based on your situation and what will allow you to grow. For me, that meant finding…

1. A safe location;
2. A place that was not visible from the street because I was going to be working late hours and did not want to be seen by passers-by;
3. A affordable, low all-inclusive rent; and
4. Big enough for me and room to grow my business.

I found it by searching real estate sites and scouting areas where I wanted to work and where my "ideal customers" wouldn't mind coming.

The perfect space for me was a small office located inside a 5-story office building. The office was next to a janitorial closet that had a sink. Using this access to water, I was able to have a shampoo bowl installed. Once I had access to water - - the rest was easy. I purchased a used station and 2 dryers. I still had all of my equipment and tools from cosmetology school - - so I was in business!

Here is a picture of my first salon location.

I signed a 3-year lease BEFORE passing the state board exam.

I had 0 clients and about the same amount of $. But this was my small beginning. With faith in God, passion for doing hair, support of my family, and loyal clients, this small room was the foundation that I stand on today. I stayed here for 6 years and then relocated to one of the most desired locations in the Memphis, Tennessee area.

Starting my search with the goal of finding a location that would meet my customers' needs, as well as my needs, provided the foundation that I stand on today. This is why this book is important. I wrote this to show you how I did it so that you know you can do it too.

I grew my business from a 1-room independent salon to a 6-room salon suites community and advanced training center.

8 ENCOURAGEMENT

True Story…

I had just opened my salon in 2006 and was trying to grow my clientele. Like many new beauty professionals, I had a couple of customers follow me from cosmetology school. That evening one of them had scheduled a shampoo, roller-set, and style. I was glad for the appointment and grateful that she decided to support me beyond the discounted services offered at the cosmetology school. She was my only appointment that evening. After working on her for 4 hours I had made $55.

Before she paid me, I went into the bathroom, cried, and had a brief conversation with the Lord that went something like this…

"Lord, I have just worked all day and I came here to do hair and all I made was $55? I cannot continue like this. What am I going to do?"

After that breakdown – – I took a deep breath, cleaned up my face, walked back into the room and told her the price. In my mind, that was going to be my last day. I WAS DONE!!

No matter how much I loved doing hair, $55 simply was not worth the time and sacrifice away from my family.

But, to my surprise - she paid me $155!

What she did not know is that her generous tip was the reassurance I needed to NOT quit.

That $100 tip, was the confirmation I needed to continue on – – in faith - - doing what I knew I was called and anointed to do.

I drove home that night in tears. I knew (without a doubt) that through her $100 tip, God was showing me that He was my source and my supply and that I was not alone.

Not long after that, I found my niche - - Helping women dealing with hair loss. I got certified in non-surgical hair restoration with weaves, wigs, and extensions and provided these specialized services in private, one-on-one appointments.

By applying the principles and philosophies in this book, I went from 1-client $55 appointments to 1-client $500 to $1000 appointments and more - straight out of cosmetology School.

Are you just starting or been in the game for a while and you are worrying, struggling, wondering if you have what it takes? Or, are you waiting for a breakthrough and just don't know what steps to take?

Being a beauty professional is such an amazing gift. The title "Beauty Professional" says that whatever you touch is made better. I am a spiritual person and depend on the Holy Spirit to lead and guide my decisions in life and in business. I also trust Him to bless what He has placed in my care. This is what I encourage you to do.

I want you to say it with me...

I CAN DO THIS!

I AM GIFTED!

I AM CAPABLE!

I AM WORTHY!

PEOPLE NEED WHAT I HAVE!

I AM THE BEST AT WHAT I DO!

It is very important to start your day intentionally. One way to do this is through prayer.

Fresh Anointing Prayer

At the start of the day at the salon or when I'm in my car heading to the salon, or while kneeling at my station before my client arrives for their appointment, I pray this simple prayer. You have my permission to use it and modify it accordingly. Fill in the blanks with your customer's name. If you don't have any customers yet, fill in the blank with the ideal customers you will have and watch them show up.

*Dear Heavenly Father, in the name of Jesus, I come to thank
You for the anointing and gifts you have placed in my care. I thank You for
_____ today. I thank You for bringing them to me to receive from me what You have so freely given.
I ask for a fresh anointing over that which You have placed in my care.
I ask Father that what I do today not only be pleasing
to _____ but more importantly, I ask that it be pleasing to You and that
it be for our good and for Your glory.
In Jesus name,*

AMEN

About the Author

Tracey Hardaway is a wife and mother of two amazing children. She is a native Memphian and has been a licensed Cosmetologist specializing in non-surgical hair replacement for over 16 years. Tracey created Hair Candy Salon, Your Extension Suite in 2006. In 2018, she opened PRN Salon Suites located in Germantown, Tennessee, to provide a Place, Resource, and Network for beauty professionals to own and operate their businesses surrounded by fellow creative professionals.

She has styled many extraordinary women and coached some brilliant beauty professionals in business and brand development

She is the CEO of Tracey Hardaway & Company where she provides next steps education, information, and inspiration to new beauty professionals so that they can start their careers with confidence. She conducts hands-on workshops teaching DIY website development and advanced hair weaving and extension techniques. She provides bespoke services for her loyal clients.

This book shares her journey from beauty school to owning her own salon and how (regardless of time/years of experience) new beauty pros and anyone who has a passion beyond their "day job" can and should be the bosses they know they are.

www.ingramcontent.com/pod-product-compliance
Lightning Source LLC
Chambersburg PA
CBHW040252220526
45473CB00001B/459